Limitless
Leadership

D1566123

Limitless Leadership

FIND YOUR DRIVE TO THRIVE

Tom Healy

© 2016 by Tom Healy
All rights reserved.

ISBN: 069271541X
ISBN-13: 9780692715413
Library of Congress Control Number: 2016941898
Reach Your Vision Publishing, Scottsdale, AZ

Dedication

This book is dedicated to my favorite leader: my mom. As a single mother, she worked tirelessly to provide me with an unbelievable childhood. She bought me my first car, sent me on amazing trips, put me through college, gave me countless opportunities to succeed, and loved me unconditionally. Many of the lessons I've learned are from firsthand observations of her kindness, toughness, work ethic, and perseverance.

Foreword

We constantly hear the word leadership being thrown around. People say you'll never get far if you're not a leader. But what if you're not a natural leader, or what if you are but you don't know how to use these skills in the most effective way?

I believe we all have the opportunity to make a big impact in our communities, our careers, and our personal lives as leaders, but due to limiting beliefs and fear many become blind to this ability. I only wish there had been a book like *Limitless Leadership* when I went through a devastating setback in the fall of 2008.

As a kid, did you ever play the game *"Would you rather?"* I know I did, and I always remember one of the most-asked questions was *"Would you rather go Deaf or Blind?"* At the time I never imagined that one of these would become my reality during my sophomore year of college.

At 19, I was your typical San Diego State University sophomore - friends, sports, fraternity and most importantly, perfect 20/20 vision. Then it happened with no warning, no time to prepare - life began to blur. Over two short months I lost central vision in my right eye, followed closely by my left. The diagnosis: a rare genetic disorder called Leber's Hereditary Optic Neuropathy (LHON), a disease with no treatment and no cure.

At first, I was told by doctors to drop out of college. It seemed that losing my sight meant forfeiting my life. I quickly fell into a deep depression, convinced that I would forever be a burden, labeled as "damaged goods," and limited by my disability. But I soon learned that my ability to succeed was stronger than my disability, and that with every challenge comes an opportunity for greatness.

Fortunately, I had surrounded myself well. With the support of the team around me and through perseverance and hard work, I learned to become a leader. A year after losing my sight, with my dad as my guide, we were invited to compete in the World Blind Golf Championship - and won! My fraternity brother and I created an annual fundraising bike ride that has raised over $200,000 for LHON research. When I wanted to drop out of college, one of my best friends encouraged me to come back to school by taking the same classes as me my first semester back to facilitate the process of becoming a blind student. Thanks to his support I graduated with a degree in Business Entrepreneurship. I was named *Challenged Athlete of the Year* by the San Diego Hall of Champions, and featured on CNN.com, MTV's True Life, ESPN.com and ABC 20/20. I developed into a leader, while I was changing perceptions of disability.

Now looking back on that childhood game, I've realized that the right answer to that question was never really "Blind" or "Deaf." The correct answer was always "either one, because no matter what, with a good team around me, I will always persevere and succeed."

Don't worry, you don't have to go through a traumatic life experience to become a leader. Tom Healy and the other leaders included in his book *Limitless Leadership* have done the hard work of going through setbacks, trials, and obstacles in order to extract the leadership skills and principles you need to know.

I've gotten to know Tom through our work as speakers with the CAMPUSPEAK agency. He's one of those rare people who are genuinely true to who they are every day. I'm inspired by how hard he works, and by his clear desire to help others succeed. If you're searching for leadership practices for your daily life, I highly encourage you to read this book because many of these answers you're seeking lie in the pages ahead.

Jeremy Poincenot

Inspirational Speaker

2010 World Blind Golf Champion

U.S. National B-2 Blind Golf Champion

San Diego, CA

www.JeremyPoincenot.com

Preface

My passion is for helping young leaders reach their extraordinary potential. I appreciate you taking the time to read this book; I promise it will help you thrive as a leader. The truth about leadership is that we are all called on to lead whether we want to or not. Leadership starts with our ability to lead our own lives and then transcends to our ability to positively impact the people and community around us. You'll find on the following pages my personal stories, stories from well-known leaders, and the integration of proven leadership theories. The goal is for you to have a strong understanding of leadership as well as specific ways to lead at a high level. The lessons in this book apply not only to leading yourself but also to leading within an organization, career, team, family, friendship, romantic relationship, and anything else you can imagine. I look forward to sharing information that will empower you to make a lasting impact on yourself and on those around you. This book isn't just about understanding leadership; it is also about doing leadership.

Tom Healy

tom@tom-healy.com

Facebook, Twitter, Instagram & LinkedIn: TomHealySays

Contents

Introduction

'd like to share a little bit about myself and why I wrote this book so that you understand my experiences and how they have shaped the words that follow. I have also found that by openly sharing your experiences and being willing to make yourself vulnerable, you develop far deeper connections with people and accomplish more as a leader.

I was born in Pittsburgh, Pennsylvania, and raised by my mom, who is the best leader I know. Assisting in my upbringing were the other two most important people in my life: my grandfather and my aunt. The lessons I learned from them as a child shaped who I have become, and I attribute many of my best qualities directly to how they carry themselves in everything they do. Many of our qualities, characteristics, and views are shaped by whom we surround ourselves with; it is critical to always surround yourself with the best possible people in life. I was fortunate to be raised by amazing individuals who taught me important lessons and selflessly provided me with a beautiful childhood.

Growing up I faced a lot of adversity, just like most children. My challenges included a lousy relationship with my father, fear of rejection, getting cut from sports teams, being scared to eat in front of girls, failures at dating, behavioral issues in school, physical insecurities, and other difficulties that seemed huge at the time. As hard as those things feel growing up, it is important to keep things in perspective and realize that it could have been worse, as there are those that face obstacles far greater than whatever we may have faced. Ultimately, one of two things happens as a result of this childhood adversity: you either become wiser and stronger because of it or continue to let it bother and define you for the rest of your life. I've seen too many people who hold on to this adversity and let it negatively affect them. They feel sorry for themselves and make excuses for their behavior as an adult because of it. Do yourself a favor and learn from your challenges; work through them, and do not let them define you.

I was bitten by the entrepreneurial bug at an early age and was constantly trying to create and sell things. I firmly believe that throughout our lives we should always be either creating something or selling something; we should all be entrepreneurs in our own way. This isn't about being greedy; you can give away all of the proceeds to charity if you'd like. This is about your ability to tap into your potential, because you never know what can come of it. After all, creativity tends to energize the brain. Throughout this book you'll read stories of great leaders who have had an unbelievable impact on the world. My early experiences in entrepreneurship certainly played a large part in me eventually owning a business, writing books, and having a continual drive to explore new opportunities. My first entry into entrepreneurship was when I was twelve years old. I created a professional-wrestling newsletter online via e-mail, something that was relatively cutting edge at the time. Through a variety of marketing efforts, I was able to build a subscriber list of thousands of wrestling fans, host weekly chats, do Q&A sessions, and constantly come up with new ways to engage my "fans." It was an absolute blast, and I learned a ton from doing it. Little did they know it was a pudgy twelve-year-old with acne on the other end of the computer.

During my first two years of high school I took classes on television production with the idea of making a career out of it. At the end of my sophomore year, the teacher who taught these classes asked to speak with me, which I was thrilled about because I assumed it was going to be a positive conversation. A funny thing happened, though. He told me in his blunt style that I wasn't very good at television production, that it was far too difficult to succeed in it if you weren't great at it, and that I should consider something else, such as business. I immediately felt as though I had been hit by a bus, since this is what I had assumed I would be doing professionally someday and what I had invested the past two years of my life in studying. I didn't immediately realize it, but it turned out to be excellent advice that I was much better off for having heard. Too often nowadays, children are shielded from negativity, which ends up causing far more harm than hearing the truth would. If he had told me I was great and given me the "dream big" talk, with some "you can be anything" sprinkled in, then I would have been absolutely screwed.

Looking back, I realized that he was 100 percent right. I wasn't good at the production side of television, and I'd have been miserable doing it, because nobody enjoys doing something he or she isn't good at. He gave me honest feedback and pointed me in the right direction. I ended up loving my business classes, having awesome teachers, and changing the trajectory of my life. For the first time, I truly felt as though I was doing something that I loved *and* was good at; it was an exhilarating feeling. The lesson here: don't be stubborn, be willing to accept honest feedback, and adjust accordingly. You have to know when to accept feedback, which I did in high school because my teacher was an expert in television production and I ultimately knew he was right. Other times you can politely decline feedback, which, as you'll see, I've also had to do at times. Rather than feeling sorry for myself, I viewed this as an opportunity to head in a better direction. When facing adversity, leaders do not make excuses or get defensive; they take responsibility and fix the problem.

I attended college at Ohio University (OU), which was an incredible experience. I truly enjoyed every second of it. The smartest thing I did at OU was to get involved in a variety of leadership organizations and take on as many leadership roles as I could in those organizations. I strongly believe that a college campus should be a training ground for the real world. It should be a place in which you surround yourself with a wide variety of people, take on a ton of outside-the-classroom experiences, and do everything you can to learn valuable life skills. You should not rely solely on your classes to prepare you for life after college, or else you will have a blank resume and lack many of the real-world skills it takes to succeed. Becoming a leader within organizations I was passionate about felt the same as taking those first business classes in high school; I felt like I was truly at my best and couldn't get enough of it.

Three days after college graduation I moved to Arizona, a place I thought would be a blast to live in for a couple of years. Fast forward a decade later; I'm still in Arizona, absolutely love it, and have no plans to ever leave. I believe too many young people focus so much on finding a job that they lose sight of what is more important at the time: picking a place that they'd love to live in. Plenty of career opportunities, especially entry-level positions, exist in virtually every city in the country so pick the place you believe you can thrive and then find a great career opportunity in that city. I wanted sunshine, outdoor activities, and golf all year long.

I found the right place for those things, and only then did I worry about finding the right career opportunity. You will absolutely work harder and be happier if you choose the right environment in which to live.

A few years after college graduation I hit that inevitable wall (which most of you will experience or have already experienced), at which point you wonder what you are doing professionally and think about how it isn't fulfilling. I was in a situation in which I worked for myself (which I loved), was advising people on their finances (which I didn't mind), and was fighting rush-hour traffic in a suit and tie (which I hated). Through a wild series of events, I was blessed with the opportunity to transition into something I was far more passionate about. I wrote my first book, *The Course They Forgot to Offer*, and was fortunate to start a new career speaking to college students around the country. I put everything I had into this opportunity and have never looked back. In the following pages, I'll share stories from this journey and what I have learned along the way. Looking back now, I can see that the biggest lesson from that entire experience was that when you see an incredible opportunity, you should jump all over it and make it happen.

Over the years, I have had the unbelievable pleasure of traveling the entire country, speaking to well over one hundred thousand people, doing strategic planning for Fortune 500 companies, consulting the US Navy, writing books, creating online learning programs, being a keynote speaker at amazing leadership conferences, and so many other awesome experiences. I believe it is important when reviewing someone's life to find key lessons, common themes, and an overall moral of that person's story. So what is the moral of my story? If you had known me growing up, you'd have probably thought I was far more likely to be sweeping the floors at Harvard than getting the opportunity to speak to executives there in my midtwenties. The reason for any success I've had is that I've been fortunate to surround myself with great people, learn as much as I can, work exceptionally hard, and persevere through all the challenges life has thrown my way.

I wrote this book because I believe we all have extraordinary potential inside of us. Many people go through life, however, without ever coming close to reaching their potential. I strongly believe that to thrive in this world you must take ownership of your life; you cannot passively sit back waiting for things to happen. You take ownership by leading yourself and those around you. Leadership is a critical skill for achieving success, but it is not being taught well enough or often enough. My hope for this book is that, after reading it, you deeply understand leadership and are then able to do it at a high level. We all have the potential within us to thrive as leaders in everything we do.

What Is Limitless Leadership?

imitless Leadership is a concept that I developed over the course of a decade of working with young leaders. I've had the opportunity to work with thousands of young leaders, to research leadership, to study successful leaders, and to draw from my own leadership experiences. I have personally observed everything from awful to amazing leadership. One of the key lessons I've learned is that everyone has an unbelievable amount of potential inside of them, but without the right series of events it often never emerges. Limitless Leadership is about all young leaders having the ability to thrive in everything they do so that they are able to improve themselves, those around them, and everything they are involved in. Leadership starts with our ability to lead our own lives and then transcends to our ability to positively impact the people and community around us.

Limitless Leadership means accepting that you are a leader, determining what drives you, and having a willingness to thrive rather than just survive, because we all have extraordinary potential inside us.

Accept that you are a leader. It may sound silly to say this, but you can't be a leader until you embrace being one. Leadership may sound scary, but it really isn't. Anyone can do it at a high level, and there is nothing wrong with "learning on the fly." If you have integrity and work hard, you are well on your way, but you'll want to first embrace being a leader.

Determine what drives you. Each of us is passionate about certain things; the quicker you can connect to what those passions are, the more powerful you will be. You should constantly be trying to determine what you are passionate about, what problems you want to solve, who you want to help, and how you can add value to people, causes, and organizations. We are all far more dangerous as leaders when we connect with what drives us, because we inevitably work harder and are more productive when we are involved with the things we care about. Allow your passions to drive your leadership of yourself and others.

Have a willingness to thrive rather than just survive. The world is far more competitive now than it has ever been, which means that doing the bare minimum simply isn't good enough. Be willing to not only take risks but embrace risk; leave your comfort zone rather than just doing the bare minimum to get by. You don't need to be in charge of everything you are involved with, but you should try to give your absolute best to whatever you are involved with.

We all have extraordinary potential inside us. Understand that you have an unbelievable amount of potential inside of you along with a desire to extract that. The faster you tap into that potential, the faster it comes out and continues to grow. Never sell yourself short or think you can't do something; every young leader I've ever worked with has had amazing leadership potential inside of them. It is just a matter of recognizing it and channeling it outward. Leaders are able to reach their potential and help others do the same.

Biggest Leadership Myths

Often in life, things are repeated so many times that we just assume they are true, even if they are partly or completely false. I've continually heard a number of things said about leadership that simply are not true. I believe it is vital to share these with you early on so that you can erase these myths from your mind and understand the truth about each of them. Here are the five biggest myths I hear about leadership; I'll set the record straight on each of them.

Leadership Myth #1: Leadership is a choice. Imagine you are walking down the street and see a woman and her two children struggling to get out of a burning building. You decide to run over, get them out, and take them somewhere safe. In a moment of crisis, you would have acted with courage and done the right thing, which would certainly cause people to commend you for your leadership in the situation. Did you technically have a choice? Sure you did, but, in reality, any decent person would have rescued that family. I can't imagine you'd witness that scene and keep walking.

We are faced with countless times in life in which we need to be a leader whether we want to be or not, such as in challenging situations with our siblings, children, friends, partners, careers, organizations, and many others. We are all called on to be leaders; it is how you act in those difficult times that ultimately determines your ability to be a leader. Don't walk through life wondering whether you are a leader, but rather accept that you need to be a leader in certain situations and then focus on doing your absolute best.

Leadership Myth #2: People are born leaders. Research continues to prove that people are not born leaders but are shaped by their experiences in life and by those individuals around them. We are not born hardwired to either be a leader or not be a leader. Those who attribute someone as a born leader are lying; the person in question wasn't born a great leader but rather became that way through interactions with certain people and through a series of events in their lives. If you want to become a great leader, it is 100 percent within your control to do so. It wasn't predetermined one way or the other when you were born. You can quickly become a great leader by reading leadership books, gaining leadership experience, and surrounding yourself with people who have strong leadership traits.

It is easy to make the excuse that you don't have any opportunities to lead, but you can immediately change this. By volunteering for a local organization that works with children, you can put yourself in a position to have a group of impressionable youngsters looking at you and wanting to learn from you and be led by you. What a great way to help others while learning how to lead! This experience will give you tangible leadership experience that is transferable to other leadership opportunities. One of my first leadership experiences was volunteering with a best friend as a youth basketball coach. It made us feel great to give back, and it gave us the opportunity to lead ten other people, make difficult decisions, challenge and push others to improve, and gain valuable leadership experience. The setting is irrelevant; just find one that you have a passion for. President John Quincy Adams summed it up well, saying, "If your actions inspire others to dream more, learn more, do more and become more, you are a leader."

Leadership Myth #3: Leaders are assertive and elected. Too often people assume that leaders are elected and that these elected individuals must be assertive. The incorrect implication here is that someone who is not elected cannot lead and that someone who is unassertive cannot lead. Leaders come in all shapes and sizes; leadership isn't strictly something for someone who is elected and assertive. Leaders can emerge from anywhere. For example, a leader could be a member of an organization who takes the initiative to do something despite not being elected to an official position or who just shows up to a charitable organization and lends a helping hand.

Leaders can also lead in a wide range of ways, not just by being loud, assertive, boisterous, and aggressive. At the core of leadership is someone helping himself or others accomplish something. If assertiveness isn't one of your qualities, certainly such helping can be done using other traits. You'll see leadership experts talk a lot about kindness, compassion, and treating others with respect. These are all important, but what it really boils down to are just the four words that my college commencement speaker told us to never forget: "Don't be a jerk."

Leadership Myth #4: Diplomas are critical. A few days before I went off to college, I happened to be talking to a complete stranger who gave me an incredible piece of advice. He said, "Don't let your classes get in the way of your real education." As I continued to get involved in organizations on campus and take on more leadership roles in those organizations, I never lost sight of the fact that I learned far more from leadership experiences, internships, and mentors than I did from anything out of a textbook taught by a professor.

Employers don't care much about where you went to school. They care about your skill set and whether you can produce results for them, and they place a premium on those with leadership skills. What is critical is what you learn, who you learn from, how hard you work, and what leadership experiences you have. Focus on opportunities to join great organizations, obtain meaningful professional opportunities, and work your absolute hardest every chance you get. If degrees from certain schools were critical, the world's most successful people would all be Ivy League educated and have advanced degrees; this is certainly far from reality. It is fascinating how little correlation there is between where you went to school and your propensity to be a great leader.

From my consulting work with companies to help them recruit, develop, and retain top young talent, I can tell you that organizations are far less focused on where you went to school and are instead more focused on your skills and past experiences. High-school guidance counselors obsess over lists of colleges and how these colleges are ranked as though it is somehow an indicator of future success or reflective of the happiness you'll experience on a given campus. If these school rankings were so critical, then every corporate recruiter would have them pinned to the wall in their office, which they do not. If you have a strong resume, great experiences, and relevant real-world skills, you will be fine. But if you lack those and believe your diploma will carry you through your career, you are in for a tough lesson. Organizations want you to produce results; that is what matters in the real world.

Leadership Myth #5: Luck and advantages are important. Do you know who says that successful people are lucky and got that way only because they had certain advantages? People who aren't successful. If you look at leaders you admire, start from the beginning of their journey to success, and I can guarantee you that a prevalent theme is that they worked exceptionally hard and most likely weren't handed much. Regardless of where people start off, the cream rises to the top and the hardest workers end up being the "lucky" ones. If you want to be a great leader, simply work hard and continue to improve yourself. Those who rely on getting lucky or waiting for an advantage usually do just that; they wait and wait for something to happen, and it never does. We all create our own opportunities in life, and great leaders take the initiative to create their own "luck." You will see throughout this book how many people didn't start in a great spot but worked their way out of challenging situations and ultimately persevered to achieve unbelievable accomplishments.

One of the most harmful things that society can do is allow people to feel like victims and spend time feeling sorry for themselves. Instead, we should push them to just work their way out of whatever challenges or disadvantages they face. For example, most people in our society would say that growing up poor is a significant disadvantage, Yet, you look at the world's most successful people, and many grew up dirt poor. Rather than feel sorry for themselves, they simply used their difficult childhoods as fuel to work even harder, do everything in their power to succeed, and ultimately create better adulthoods. I know plenty of people who grew up wealthy and had lots of "advantages" yet have struggled as adults; all that wealthy upbringing led to was a sense of entitlement, a lack of work ethic, and no appreciation for what it takes to achieve success. As I said, the cream rises to the top regardless of where you start, as we all control our own destiny. Do you want to make an impact as a leader? Go do it.

How to Thrive
as a Leader

As you can probably tell by now, I am a straight shooter and directly communicate my feelings. The heart and soul of this book are the following six key points. If you understand these and actively implement them in everything you do, you will thrive as a leader. Each of the six key points follows the same format, which I believe makes understanding and implementing the points much easier. There is an explanation of the trait, stories to illustrate that trait in action, a summary of the trait, and, finally, an explanation of how to implement the trait while leading yourself and leading others. When sharing educational information, I believe you should explain the concept, show it in action, and explain how to do it. I don't want you to simply understand leadership but rather understand it and be able to do it at a high level. This book isn't just about understanding leadership; it is also about actually leading.

1. Be the Hardest Worker in the Room

There may be people who have more talent than you, but there's no excuse for anyone to work harder than you do.

—Derek Jeter

Recently I was getting ready to play a round of golf with a family friend who has experienced a great deal of professional success and is a truly amazing person as well. He was in the midst of a conversation with a soon-to-be college graduate and called me over to share my best piece of advice with the student. Initially I felt a little bit of pressure to come up with a great answer, but I quickly realized the right answer is actually quite simple. I responded with, "Outwork everyone." I went on to explain that the easiest way to separate yourself and achieve success is by working harder than everyone around you. It is the easiest thing you can control, and that hard work leads to learning more, experiencing greater challenges, and moving up faster in your career. You can't control a lot of things in life, but one thing you can always control is how hard you work. After I gave this student my blunt advice, our family friend nodded his head and assured the student I was spot on because in his years of experience running companies, he had learned the value of hard work and had seen how too few people actually work hard. If you aren't willing to work hard, then there is a ceiling on what you can accomplish. If you want to thrive as a leader, make the commitment to work exceptionally hard.

During the summer after my first year of college, I had the incredible opportunity to have an internship in corporate sales for the Pittsburgh Pirates. Over the course of the summer, I would routinely be the first person in the entire organization in the building each morning. Because my internship was during the baseball season, half of the days I was there we'd have a game, which often led to late nights. The majority of my weeks involved eighty-plus hours of work. To me, it was a no-brainer to put in that level of work. I was passionate about the team, loved the work I was doing, wanted to learn as much as possible, and wanted the experience of doing as many different things as I could. I was the youngest person there, had the least experience, and had the fewest years of "education." There was no reason for me to thrive in that environment. But I consistently got great opportunities because they knew they could count on me to work exceptionally hard, and I was always there when they needed something. Throughout the summer, I took players to public appearances, hosted top corporate sponsors in the owner's box, had a postgame drink with the manager, took batting practice on the field, built multimillion-dollar sponsorship proposals, and so much more because people took notice of my work ethic and kept giving me more opportunities. In turn, I delivered on these opportunities at a high level. Going into that summer I knew I could control one thing: to be the hardest worker in the room. I did that every day. How did I feel physically and emotionally that summer after eighty-hour weeks? I was energized because I was passionate about what I was doing. We are virtually unstoppable and have exponentially more energy when we are able to do something we genuinely enjoy.

As I progressed through college, I continued to get involved in more leadership organizations and did my best to lead at a high level in each of them. Halfway through my senior year I had already lined up the city I was going to live in and the career opportunity I would be pursuing. As a result, I was told many times how lucky I was. What I wanted to say was that I wasn't lucky at all but was in this position because I had worked harder than anyone around me and consequently created opportunities for myself. Instead of logging ten-hour sessions of PlayStation, I had stepped up as a leader in a variety of organizations. Instead of sleeping in until noon, I had awakened at seven o'clock and begun working hard no matter how late I had been out the night before. When you add up all those additional hours of leadership experience over a four-year period, you realize there is a massive gap between the experience of a hard worker like me and that of the average student. The top young leaders that I have interacted with over the years had no advantages or luck. Just like me, they simply outworked everyone around them and continually took on additional leadership opportunities every chance they had. What holds true on a college campus also holds true in the real world. Imagine the massive gap between those that spend their twenties hustling and those that do the bare minimum to get by. This gap only widens as the years go on.

In addition to working hard, I cannot emphasize enough the importance of lifelong learning. Two of the common qualities of the most successful people I've ever met is that they are constantly curious about the world around them and work hard to learn new things on a daily basis. I'm amused when I see someone that is packed with arrogance, believes they know it all, and has no work ethic; extremely successful people are driven to improve through learning. Great leaders know they have a lot to learn and will continue learning how to improve their leadership skills every day. There is zero excuse not to continue learning, as you can google just about anything and learn about it within seconds. President John F. Kennedy may have said it best when he said that "leadership and learning are indispensable to each other."

As many people know, the Beatles once got their big break on *The Ed Sullivan Show*. Those telling the story of the band's success often start with this appearance and the subsequent massive popularity that came of it. But those that start the tale with this appearance miss the entire point of the story, which is that they had played over one thousand times before they experienced any success at all. There are plenty of bands who would have quit along the way and not had the work ethic to persevere, but they kept playing until their hard work paid off. Does this mean that every band that keeps playing will make it big? Of course not. It is important to continue to get better, and the right opportunities need to present themselves. But without that work ethic you have virtually no chance of success. I'm sure at various times they all wanted to give up, but they were able to stick together and lead themselves to success.

Back in the 1970s, an aspiring young comedian who was attending Queens College would take the train weekly into New York City and sit in a comedy club for hours. He hoped to be able to tell a few jokes to a drunk audience late in the night during an open mic portion of the evening. He continued doing this every week, some nights never even getting a chance to be on the stage at all, until he finally had the opportunity for his own segment and eventually to get compensated for his efforts. Many aspiring comedians, musicians, artists, and others have similar stories of spending years trying to catch a break. And for each one who did catch a break there are thousands who did not. Just for people to reach the point at which they catch a break they have to work exceptionally hard, both to force themselves into the opportunity for that break and to then deliver a quality performance that will lead to the next break.

This aspiring comedian was Jerry Seinfeld, who would eventually receive opportunities on bigger stages; all of his hard work earned him a test run of a show on NBC. Fast-forward through years of hard work and perseverance, and you'll find someone who is worth over $800 million and generated seventy-six million viewers for the finale of his sitcom.

Most people look at him and think his humor is what made him successful. If that's how you view his career, then you miss the entire lesson, which is that there are thousands of folks out there just like him. He just outworked them from a young age and continued to work tirelessly as his career progressed. Do you think his work ethic rubbed off on the other actors, writers, and production people? Of course it did, and this led to one of the greatest shows in television history.

Just like people aren't born leaders, they are also not born world-class athletes. Take, for instance, Michael Jordan, who was famously cut from his high-school varsity basketball team as a sophomore. He used this as motivation, worked tirelessly, made the team as a junior, and, then, made the McDonald's All-American high-school team as a senior. This rapid ascension didn't occur because of luck, chance, a wealthy upbringing, or any reason other than just a plain old exceptional work ethic. Continuing into his college and professional career, Jordan was known for his ridiculous work ethic and would spend hours each day practicing. Away from Chicago Bulls team practices, Jordan would continue to practice on his own at his house. As time went on, his best teammate, Scottie Pippen, started joining his at-home practice sessions, and eventually the majority of the team followed suit. Jordan chose to lead his teammates by example and created a work ethic within the Chicago Bulls organization that ultimately led to six NBA championships for the team. Jordan summed it up well by saying, "Some people want it to happen, some wish it would happen, and others make it happen."

The Bottom Line: There is no substitute for hard work. Without it, you simply cannot be successful. The easiest thing for you to control is your work ethic, and when you work hard, amazing things "magically" happen.

Key Points:

- It is very difficult to thrive without working hard.
- Those who outwork everyone around them experience greater success and have a greater impact as a leader.
- You should have the drive to keep improving yourself and developing as a leader.

Leading Yourself: Focus on dominating whatever you are doing at the moment. If you work exceptionally hard at everything you do, you'll be amazed at what happens.

Leading Others: Use these stories and ones from your own life to articulate the value of hard work so you can help others understand the connection between working hard and achieving great results.

2. Have a Laser-Focused Vision

The only thing worse than being blind

is having sight but no vision.

—Helen Keller

Visions give people purpose. When leading yourself or leading others, have a laser-focused vision of what you are working toward. Have the ability to understand what the end goal is, develop a plan for how to get there, and motivate yourself or others along the way. Leadership becomes far easier when everyone knows what the vision is and why that is the vision. This is applicable whether you are leading a community event or a Fortune 500 company; the process is exactly the same. Understand where you want to end up, have a laser focus on what that destination looks like, and then develop a step-by-step plan for how to get there. If you apply this to everything you want to accomplish, you'll experience far better results. As circumstances change, you'll need to shift your vision and plans accordingly, but you never want to lose sight of what you are working toward.

Once I decided I wanted to quit what I was doing and figure out a way to speak at colleges full time, there was the inevitable lack of income. I wasn't making a dime, so what did I do for money? I borrowed it from family, friends, Visa, MasterCard, and American Express. It was the most scared I have ever been in my life by far. But I am proud that I paid it all back, and I'd do it again in a heartbeat. There was one day in particular when I was first getting started that stands out as an example of the importance of having a strong vision. I was pumping gas and swiped my debit card, which linked to my bank account. Right after I started pumping, I realized I had no idea how much money was left in my bank account. I immediately pulled up my banking app and checked the balance, and it turned out that I didn't even have enough to fill up the entire tank. I had to quickly stop pumping gas. I just stood there for a minute thinking to myself, what the hell are you doing? I literally wanted to fall to the ground and start crying.

After I gathered myself, I took a deep breath, closed my eyes, and imagined how it would feel to stand in front of a huge room packed with college students who I was able to positively impact with my words. I visualized them engaged in what I was sharing, and I felt my enthusiasm as I passionately delivered helpful information to them. If it weren't for this laser-focused vision of what I was determined to accomplish, I would have quit trying and found a real job, or I would've just sat down on that ground and started crying. My vision of how it would feel to be successful at something I was passionate about is the only reason I was able to make it through some really difficult times. I was far more depressed and scared than I ever let anyone know, but my vision for the future guided me through the challenges. I stayed focused every day on what I wanted to accomplish and eventually got there; if you don't have that vision, it will make tough times feel impossible.

As important as it is to have a laser-focused vision, it is equally important to understand what it will take to accomplish any goal that you have set for yourself. As President Barack Obama said, "We need to steer clear of this poverty of ambition, where people want to drive fancy cars and wear nice clothes and live in nice apartments but don't want to work hard to accomplish these things. Everyone should try to realize their full potential." There is no lack of dreamers in this world, but very few understand the hard work and actions it takes to accomplish their vision. Make sure that when you want something (such as a fancy car, nice clothes, and a nice apartment), you also understand what it takes to accomplish that and are willing to make it happen.

One of America's first great visionaries was Benjamin Franklin, who once famously said, "Some people die at twenty-five and aren't buried until seventy-five." Too many people in our society, even three hundred years later, simply stop trying to accomplish new things or improve their communities. When you stop trying to accomplish things, you more or less stop living, which is why it is critical to always have that next vision for what you want to accomplish. As Franklin said, "When you're finished changing, you're finished." The average life span in the 1700s was only thirty-five years old, yet Franklin lived to be eighty-four, which was an unbelievable accomplishment. I attribute his longevity to the same reasons why some people nowadays outlive the average life span: they continue to learn, stay active, surround themselves with exceptional people, and are young at heart. The following list of

Franklin's major accomplishments highlights how he continued creating new, laser-focused visions for himself and his community. He became one of the Founding Fathers of the United States, discovered key information about electricity, invented bifocals, and served as president of Pennsylvania. He epitomized someone who stayed hungry and continued developing ambitious visions.

When facing challenging circumstances, it can be difficult to develop a vision for a successful future. At the age of fourteen, a young man came home to find an eviction notice; his family was being kicked out of their home. His mother broke down in tears and said, "Where are we going to live? What are we going to do?" This young man put his family through additional stress by frequently getting in trouble with the law, including being involved in a theft ring. He eventually cleaned up his act and became a college football star with a vision of playing professionally. Unfortunately, injuries closed the door on this vision. Facing depression and an uncertain future, he committed to turning his life around; as he said, "I looked in my pocket, and I had seven bucks. Wow...In 1995, I had seven bucks in my pocket and knew two things: I'm broke as hell and one day I won't be."

This young man's new vision was to become a professional wrestler, as his father and grandfather had successfully done. After working hard to learn this craft, he morphed into "The Rock." He was the first-ever African American WWE World Heavyweight Champion and became arguably the biggest star in the history of the industry. Along the way he also found the time to write an autobiography that became a *New York Times* best seller. He then developed a new vision for himself: to morph into Dwayne Johnson, the actor. He started all over again as a rookie in Hollywood. His work ethic and determination guided him to become among Hollywood's biggest movie stars; *Time* magazine recently recognized him as one of the one hundred most influential people in the world. He also runs a successful production company, appropriately called 7 Bucks Entertainment.

Bill Gates, cofounder of Microsoft, is often commended for his business accomplishments, which have led to him being the richest man in the world. Countless books and articles have commended Gates for being a visionary due to those accomplishments, which are undoubtedly remarkable. Another vision of his may end up having a much larger impact on the world, however. As early as 1994, Gates began studying the work of philanthropists Andrew Carnegie and John D. Rockefeller with a vision in mind of shifting from businessman to philanthropist. His years of planning led to the creation, along with his wife, Melinda, of the Bill & Melinda Gates Foundation, which they have built into a charitable organization worth over $40 billion. The foundation's aims are, globally, to enhance health care and reduce extreme poverty and, in America, to expand educational opportunities and access to information technology. The lessons here are that we should be willing to build a large vision (his company) and, then, once it is reached, to look for the next vision to create (his foundation). Leaders stay hungry and are constantly looking for new opportunities. It is also important to note the wonderful impact that Bill and Melinda have made with their wealth. There are people in our society with the attitude that money and wealth are bad. In reality, though, money can be good or bad depending on who has it and what they choose to do with it.

There are countless stories from the sports world of teams with inferior talent that accomplished significant success due to the vision set forth by their head coach. None of these teams is more famous than the 1980 US Olympic men's hockey team, who, against all odds, defeated the Soviet Union in the game dubbed the "Miracle on Ice." The Soviet Union was a heavy favorite, having entered the game with a record of 27-1-1 since the 1960 Olympics and having outscored their opponents 175–44. Meanwhile, Team USA was comprised of no professional hockey players but rather of a group of amateur and collegiate players. Throughout the 1980 Olympics, Team USA head coach Herb Brooks was able to paint an extraordinary vision for his players and provide them the road map to realize it. The result of this vision was a group of unexperienced players winning an improbable gold medal. On multiple occasions, Coach

Brooks would issue the challenge to his players to "be better than you are. Set a goal that seems unattainable, and when you reach that goal, set another one even higher." When setting a vision for yourself or for an entire organization, set the bar high and aim for excellence. Too often people set goals they know they can reach because they are easily attainable and don't have to get out of their comfort zone. Challenge yourself to set your sights on wildly ambitious visions and then get to work reaching them.

The Bottom Line: Leaders have the ability to develop a laser-focused vision and winning plan for whatever they want to accomplish. They then empower either themselves or an entire team to reach that vision.

Key Points:

- Without a clear vision, you are wandering aimlessly instead of working efficiently toward what you want to accomplish.
- Most of the world's biggest accomplishments were the results of a clear vision, a plan to achieve it, and lots of hard work along the way.
- Develop ambitious visions for yourself and your organizations; complacency doesn't result in greatness.

Leading Yourself: Figure out something you want to accomplish, paint a clear picture in your mind of the end result, and then develop the specific steps it will take to achieve your vision. Also, think of how it will make you feel when you realize that vision. If you are having trouble accomplishing the goal on your own, be willing to discuss it with others and brainstorm together.

Leading Others: Work with others to craft a clear vision of what you want your organization to accomplish, create actionable items with due dates to make this happen, and work together to achieve it. Along the way, help everyone accomplish their tasks and keep the team collectively focused on the vision as challenges arise.

3. Surround Yourself with Good People

The key is to keep company only with people who up-
lift you, whose presence calls forth your best.

—Epictetus

The people you surround yourself with in life will have an undeniable effect on your success, happiness, and enjoyment. In a lot of ways, people are the only thing that truly matter in your life; on your deathbed you'll be thinking about the people you surrounded yourself with, not the flat-screen TV you purchased or a car that you drove. If your final thoughts do involve material possessions, then you probably were not able to live life to the fullest, because it is the people, not the things, in our lives and our experiences with those people that give us the greatest satisfaction. Scientific research continues to show that we gain far more happiness from experiences with people than we do from material items purchased for ourselves.

In order to reach your greatest level of happiness in life and your greatest potential as a leader, it is critical that you choose the best possible people to surround yourself with. You can accomplish small things on your own, without the help of others, but as you progress in life and have larger ambitions (improving an organization, launching a business, starting a family, raising a large sum for charity, and just about anything else), you cannot go it alone. And even if you could do it alone, who wants to?

One of the key reasons we should, as leaders, strive to surround ourselves well is that we emulate the characteristics, skills, and values of those around us. Everything we do (that is, the actions we take, the decisions we make, and the mannerisms we exhibit) are shaped by the people we spend time with. You can quickly elevate your ability as a leader by seeking out people who are doing or have done the things that you want to do at a high level. As motivational speaker Jim Rohn famously said, "You are the average of the five people you spend the most time with."

I'd like to share the relationship I had with my grandfather, who I called Pup, to reinforce the importance of surrounding yourself with good people. He was my hero, my inspiration, my best friend, and everything to me. We had such a special relationship. He once wrote down a list of everything we had experienced together, and at the bottom of the paper he wrote, "It has been a wonderful experience, thank you." And it truly had been. A lot of people throughout life have ups and downs in relationships, but ours was the absolutely perfect relationship every single day. We spoke every day. I would give him a call, and he'd enthusiastically say, "Hey, buddy!" or "My main man!" No matter how bad a day I was having, his greeting would make any pain I was experiencing immediately go away.

As a former teacher of mine so perfectly put it, "I don't know if he was more proud of you or if you were more proud of him." He constantly reinforced to me the importance of family and didn't understand why some families argued or didn't get along. As he would say, "What the hell is wrong with these people?" I learned the importance of work ethic from him, as throughout his life he set up bowling pins, hauled coal around, and worked in a grocery store. His generation didn't make excuses or expect a handout; they just worked their absolute hardest, because that's what you did in those days.

Pup was great at surrounding himself with good people; being around people truly meant everything to him. Even well into his eighties, he was hitting the local hotspots. He would sit there with a glass of wine and talk to people for hours, and everyone in the community knew him and loved him. One time I had the audacity to ask him why he never went to a certain place on Saturday nights, and he simply said, "There is no action there on Saturdays." Another time we tried to get him to leave one of his favorite spots because a blizzard was coming; my mom and aunt were worried because he had no cell phone. Finally, my mom went down there and said, "Daddy, it's time to go home because a blizzard is coming." He responded with, "No way, the Budweiser girls haven't gotten here yet!"

I truly learned so much from him. He was an inspiration to everyone, and I was blessed to have him in my life. He made me a better person, kept me grounded, made me smile when I was going through some tough times, and gave me so much happiness. Find people in your life that can do the same for you, and cherish every minute you have with them.

Special people like him make life more enjoyable and make you a much better leader because you emulate many of their best characteristics.

You never know when or how some of the most important people in your life will enter it, so always be ready when the opportunity arises to meet someone special. While still in my previous career, I had begun working on a side project, which would become my first book, *The Course They Forgot to Offer*. Late one night I was in my office working when a colleague walked up to me and asked if I could help him with a computer issue he was having. After I quickly fixed the issue, we began making small talk, which eventually led to him sharing that he was working on a book and that for the past decade he had been traveling around the world speaking. I shared with him that I was working on a book too, and he told me I was crazy if I didn't finish the book as quickly as I could and then figure out a way to begin speaking to college audiences. As soon as he said this, I instantly remembered sitting at my fraternities' leadership school a few years earlier, listening to a keynote speaker, and thinking how awesome it would be to one day have the opportunity to do that for a living. I thought to myself, someday that is going to be me up there. Sure enough, one day it was.

My colleague and I agreed to have lunch the next day, and at the end of it he offered to mentor me throughout the process of writing a book and becoming a speaker. We also agreed that we would meet every single week until I was finished writing the book. At each of these meetings I had to report to him what I had done, what I was going to do the following week, and what, if any, problems he could help me solve. So, what are the lessons here? First, had I not been working late I would have never met Tom. Keep in mind that successful people don't work the bare minimum; they go above the average worker in terms of effort and hours. Second, when you identify an opportunity to connect your strengths with your passions, you attack it with everything you have. When the light bulb went off with the realization that I could write a book to help people a little younger than I was and then travel around the country sharing that information, I dedicated an insane amount of energy to make it happen. Third, you should have mentors. Tom helped me get up and running far more quickly than I could have ever done without him. When you have the opportunity to spend time with someone like this, you should do everything in your power to make it happen and to build the best possible relationship you can. We have remained close friends, and he provided me with great feedback as I wrote this book.

Back when I had just finished my first book, I was extremely proud of it and ready to travel the country speaking. As with many things in life, it wasn't easy, and I had a tremendous amount to learn. Relatively early on in this process, I networked my way into being able to deliver a free workshop at a leadership conference. Heading into this program, I found out that the owner of the top college-speaking agency would also be in attendance at the conference, so I reached out to him. I asked if he would be willing to attend my session and meet with me afterward so that I could learn more about speaking at colleges. He gladly accepted, and I knew this was a huge opportunity. If you want to succeed at something, you should always seek out people who have done what you want to do at a high level and learn as much from them as you can. He provided me with invaluable feedback on my program and with great professional advice. We continued to stay in touch, which eventually led to him taking me under his wing and showing me how to be successful as a speaker and consultant. Fast-forward all these years later, and my relationship with David has been among the most important in my life, both personally and professionally. I continue to speak for his agency, and we also own a consulting business together that does great work for college fraternities and sororities. You never know how life will play out, but I have serious doubts that I'd have accomplished the things I have professionally had I not met David. There are plenty of successful people out there willing to help someone who is young and ambitious. Seek them out, because you truly never know what it will lead to.

Below are the key relationships you'll want to have in your life. Some of them you may already have well established, and others may be empty at the moment. Take your time in filling these voids with the right people. They may happen to come into your life, or you may seek them out because you believe you'd benefit from having a relationship with them. This isn't about the quantity; it is about the quality of these people and your relationships with them. Too often in life, we try to please everyone and measure things based on the number of "likes" we get. True satisfaction, however, is based on the depth, not the number, of our relationships. Here are key relationships to work on establishing or further developing as you improve yourself as a leader.

Yourself. It's a cliché, but it's true; when you look in the mirror, you should like what you see. Oftentimes the relationship you have with yourself is overlooked. If you think about it, though, you spend hours each day by yourself, thinking to yourself, and making internal decisions, so it is critical for your mental health that you have a good relationship with yourself.

Family. Family is interesting because it is different for everyone, and very few families are conventional these days. For example, my mom was both mother and father to me, my aunt was more like a second mom, and my Pup Pup and I were extremely close. Over the years, I have become increasingly close to my stepbrother and stepmother, both of whom are an important part of my life. Growing up, I also had a nanny who helped raise me. She was the grandmother I never had and taught me many valuable lessons at a young age. As I grew older, I became extremely close to another family that I now consider part of my own family. Relationships with family are never easy, but they are well worth the work and are important to your personal and professional development.

Friends. Life can be challenging, so having a strong support system of deep friendships will help you persevere through the bad times and enjoy the good times. I cannot tell you how many times over the years I've faced adversity and leaned heavily on my friends. No matter what challenges I face, I know that I've got a group of people who have my back and will do everything in their power to help me.

As an example, I've been incredibly blessed to have a best friend who has always been there for me and provided guidance to me on every major issue, challenge, and obstacle I've faced over the past fifteen years. It is an incredible feeling to have that level of support in your life, and I highly recommend you find people who will do that for you and who you will do that for. When we are at our best, friends make life more fun; when we are at our worst, they give us a safety net to fall back on and help protect us.

Acquaintances. In addition to having close friends, it is also important to have people in your life you can spend enjoyable time with socially. Life is simply more fun when you share it with other people, and not every friend needs to be a close one.

Teachers. I have been blessed to have some amazing people over the years as teachers. I've stayed in touch with many of them because they had such a huge impact on my development as a leader. My second-grade teacher was the reason I found a passion for writing. She was able to take a loudmouthed kid and channel his energy toward creative writing, recognizing his strengths rather than just casting him off as another misbehaving student.

In middle school, a lousy time in most kids' lives, I dealt with a whole host of issues but was fortunate to have a teacher who refused to quit on me and did countless things to boost my self-esteem. I will forever be grateful to him for that. At a pivotal time in my life, he was a much-needed positive male role model who encouraged me and made sure I was on the right path during a time when I could have easily not been.

In eighth grade, I had a miserable homeroom teacher who was causing me issues and eventually kicked me out of her homeroom for absolutely no good reason. Fortunately, I had an amazing English teacher who took me into her homeroom, showed me what kindness really was, and helped to reinvigorate my passion for writing and creating content through a daily sports column that she encouraged me to write as a project for her class.

I was also blessed by a group of business teachers in high school who were catalysts for me hitting my academic stride, figuring out that business was the perfect future for me, and finding the entrepreneurial spirit that has led me to where I am today. Teachers can have an unbelievable impact on your development as a leader; gravitate toward the right ones and let them help you reach your potential.

Mentors. Find people who are either doing or have done the types of things, personally or professionally, that you want to do. Mentors are individuals who can help you accomplish the things you want to because they have already done them at a high level. Some mentors will stay in your life for years, and others will be in it for only a short time. These mentor relationships come in different forms but can be invaluable. Successful people will almost always be willing to help you, as an ambitious young leader, as long as you ask them for their help. Mentors are not your personal cheerleaders. The best ones are brutally honest, challenge you, and put you in a position to succeed.

Professional colleagues. It will help your ongoing development as a leader if you have relationships with people who understand your professional life and can help you grow in your career or industry. It is important to have the right people giving you career advice. Sometimes this advice can come from family, friends, and partners, but other times those aren't the best people to be giving you guidance in that area. I am very careful about who I solicit professional advice from and who I develop professional relationships with because I recognize that most people aren't uniquely qualified to help me in this area.

Romantic partners. Many great leaders will attribute much of their success to having a rock-solid partner who makes them a better person and makes the ups and downs of life much smoother than they would be alone.

Determine the types of people you want to spend your time with. Their characteristics could include being ambitious, honest, positive, loyal, friendly, funny, authentic, optimistic, charitable, selfless, interested in lifelong learning, great at listening, or other characteristics good people tend to have. Never take for granted the amazing people you surround yourself with. Leaders have the ability to make others feel important by providing them with positive reinforcement, recognizing their accomplishments, and showing appreciation of them.

One of the characteristics I have noticed in many successful leaders is their ability to develop new relationships and bring people together. As a leader, figure out ways to meet new people, connect people, recruit people, and bring people together. It will not only benefit them but also help you expand your network and the reach you have as a leader. It is amazing what you can accomplish by bringing people together and building bridges between like-minded organizations.

Throughout the process of writing this book, I reached out to a number of people I trust and asked them for their honest feedback; their collective responses made it significantly better. When you surround yourself with good people, they will not only be there for you but also give you feedback that makes whatever you are doing better. Have a willingness to ask those around you for honest feedback and have an open mind about what they have to say. You won't do everything they suggest (nor should you), but it will make you better to listen to their feedback.

Here's an interesting question to ponder: can we learn from bad people? In my personal experience, the answer is an overwhelming yes. It can be as simple as looking at someone you don't admire and doing the opposite of what that person has done. Growing up, I did not have a great relationship with my father and had to look elsewhere for positive male role models, which I was fortunate enough to find in the form of some incredible men. Someone once told me that she doubted my ability to be a good father because of the poor job my father had done; hearing that from someone I cared about hurt—a lot. I had previously given thought to this, and so my response was a forceful one. I said that I was unbelievably determined to become a great father because of how poorly mine had done, and I would do the complete opposite of all the things he had done. Can you learn from bad examples of leadership? Absolutely.

The Bottom Line: The impact you have as a leader is highly dependent on the quality of people you surround yourself with. Focus on finding good people to fill the various types of relationships you need to thrive.

Key Points:

- The people you surround yourself with will have a large effect on your personal and professional life, as you will begin to emulate their characteristics.
- Constantly surround yourself with high-quality people who assist in your development as a leader.
- Be a connector who meets new people and connects good people and organizations with each other.

Leading Yourself: Pick someone you want to have a deeper relationship with, seek that person out, and start spending time with him or her.

Leading Others: Start being more deliberate about connecting people and organizations who you think would mutually benefit from knowing each other.

4. Be Authentic 24-7

Do what you feel in your heart to be right,

for you'll be criticized anyway.

—Eleanor Roosevelt

Your confidence as a leader will continue to improve as you become more comfortable in your own skin. Leaders often mistakenly try to be everything to everyone, changing their demeanor on the fly depending on the situation and acting the way they think they should act based on their specific role in a situation. In addition to being your authentic self, as a leader you should create a culture within the organizations you are involved with that allows everyone to feel comfortable being themselves.

Keep in mind that certain situations require a different level of professionalism than do others. The language and subject matter you use at a bar or sporting event might not be appropriate for a professional environment. As a mature adult, you should determine which settings require the more professional version of your authentic self and which settings are appropriate for a more relaxed version of your authentic self. It is perfectly acceptable to maintain your genuine authenticity but adapt your authentic personality based on the setting. What you want to avoid is needing to radically change your behavior from one setting to another.

As a leader it is impossible to agree with or please everyone, but leaders have the ability to understand and respect everyone's opinions while still being their authentic selves. Too often nowadays in our society, people have their feelings on certain issues and cannot fathom how anyone could possibly see the world differently. But the world is not black and white, people have different views for different reasons, and intelligent leaders are able to understand a wide range of perspectives. You will be a better person for respecting all views instead of saying "he is dumb" or "she is wrong" without at least understanding the other person's perspective and trying to put yourself in his shoes to feel what he feels. Leaders have the ability to be the "adult in the room" rather than thinking their own views can be the only correct ones. You can certainly be respectful of others, understand their perspectives, and feel what they feel while remaining authentic to who you are. Leaders also understand that conflict and disagreement amongst people and within organizations can be positive as long as all parties are respectful of each other and use it as an opportunity to learn or improve.

By the time my senior year of college approached, I had put together a pretty robust résumé. I had been involved in various organizations, a wide range of leadership experiences, a club sport, and great internships, and I had done well academically. Nothing was handed to me, and I wasn't the brightest person on campus. I just worked my butt off from the first day I arrived in Athens, Ohio. As a junior, my focus started to shift from résumé building to actually finding a career. In our college of business, we had a certification program for sales through the Sales Centre. I thought it would be worthwhile to do this program since I was pursuing a career in sales. The program had an application and interview process in order to get accepted, so I applied and went through an interview with one of our business professors. My application was exceptionally strong because of all my related experience, and the interview could not have gone better. I walked away feeling 100 percent confident that I would get into the program.

After a few weeks, I received the e-mail with the results; I didn't get in. I was in complete shock and immediately scheduled a meeting with the director of the entire program (someone different from the person who had interviewed me) to find out what had happened. When I sat in the director's office, he told me he was surprised I didn't get into the program and reviewed the feedback from the professor who had rejected me. The key negative against me was that I was "too polished" and that my responses to questions were very quick and confident. Well, of course I was polished, quick, and confident; I had sales and leadership experience, had been through similar interviews before, and had quick answers for all the questions since they were the same boring questions asked in virtually every interview.

I share this story because it presents an interesting dilemma: should you adapt who you are based on this kind of feedback or continue to be your authentic self? I certainly do not advocate disrespecting people or rejecting negative feedback every time you receive it, but you always need to consider the source of the feedback before you decide what to do with it. The feedback that I was given came from a college professor who had very little real-world sales experience, so I made the decision that I was not going to compromise my authenticity or make a dramatic shift in how I carried myself simply because of her opinion. Had this feedback come from someone with more impressive credentials, I would have taken it more seriously. The lesson here is that when you are given negative feedback, consider the source. Sometimes you should take it to heart, but other times you should take it with a grain of salt.

In first grade, I had a teacher that kept moving my seat because I was too energetic and couldn't sit still. In today's overmedicated society, I would have been told I had ADHD and been given a bottle of pills to "fix" the problem. Fortunately for me, my "medicine" was a second-grade teacher who recognized my strength in writing and channeled my energy toward writing stories about anything my imagination could come up with. She taught me an important lesson, as she did with all of her students during her teaching career. She showed that it was possible to identify her students' passions and strengths and channel their energy toward those while still allowing them to remain their authentic selves. Great leaders are able to identify the strengths in everyone they work with and create opportunities for them to utilize those authentic strengths for the improvement of themselves or their organizations.

One of my pet peeves is watching someone trying to deliver a performance or a scripted presentation to an audience instead of communicating authentically with the audience. One of the best compliments I have ever received came when I first started speaking at colleges; after delivering a program, I started interacting one-on-one with a student who had some questions for me. At the end of our conversation, he looked at me and said, "Dude, you are like the same person now that you were when you were speaking." I laughed and asked him what he meant by that. He went on to say that speakers typically act differently onstage than they do offstage. I never forgot this interaction because it is a great reminder of the importance of being authentic 24-7 and of not having different onstage and offstage personas. Communicating authentically in every setting in which you find yourself will serve you well.

It isn't easy to be consistent as a leader. We all have a tendency to want to act differently depending on our role in any given situation. A classic example of this is the Stanford Prison Experiment, conducted in 1971. In this experiment, twenty-four men were selected to participate; half of them were to be "prisoners" and the other half were to be "prison guards." The environment, clothing, and rules were all set up to mimic a real-life prison. Each of the prisoners was brought in like a typical prisoner would be, and the prison guards had an orientation to make sure they understood the role of a prison guard. The original plan was for this experiment to last for seven to fourteen days, but it had to be stopped after only six days due to a combination of depressed prisoners and abusive prison guards. Even though all twenty-four men in the experiment were normal citizens, once they were assigned their roles they still acted like either a prisoner or a guard despite not actually being one and despite knowing they were involved in an experiment. This goes to show that we all have a tendency to act the way we think we are supposed to act given the role, title, or position that we have. The lesson to learn here is that, as a leader, you should resist the urge to change into someone you're not just because you think an individual in your situation is supposed to act a certain way. For instance, you may feel that the president of an organization must be strong and assertive, but if you are more the kind and caring type, then stick to being your authentic self. It will serve you well, and people will appreciate your authenticity.

In addition to being yourself, you should also continually strive to be both honest and transparent. As the famous author Mark Twain once said, "If you tell the truth, you don't have to remember anything." His point here is simple: it is a lot easier to just tell the truth and be an open book rather than to say what you think people want to hear. Part of being authentic

24-7 is being transparent and honest as a leader in whatever you are doing. Are there times when, as a leader, you will need to put an optimistic spin on a challenging situation? Of course there are, and as a leader you should strive to remain optimistic in difficult situations, but you can certainly do that while still telling the truth. You will develop stronger relationships with those around you when they know they can trust you.

Life is far too short to be anyone but yourself. Being your authentic self, however, can often come with challenges. Ellen DeGeneres was thriving, with a highly rated network sitcom, when she decided to announce that she was gay. In her words, "I had everything I'd hoped for, but I wasn't being myself. So I decided to be honest about who I was. It was strange: the people who loved me for being funny suddenly didn't like me for being...me." Regarding her show, she explained, "The network canceled the show after six years without even telling me; I read it in the paper. The phone didn't ring for three years. I had no offers. Nobody wanted to touch me at all. Yet I was getting letters from kids who almost committed suicide, but didn't, because of what I did. And I realized that I had a purpose. And it wasn't just about me, and it wasn't about celebrity." Despite the tough times, she eventually persevered and developed a hit talk show that has focused on inspirational stories and helping others. She continually explains how happy she is that she embraced who she really was, and she has made it a goal to help others do the same, regardless of what challenges they are facing. Her inspirational message teaches us that a huge weight is lifted when you embrace who you are. Those who love you will still love you, and those who are against you were never truly with you in the first place. It takes courage to be your authentic self, but it is worth it.

Some of the most fascinating things you can learn from are commencement speeches because they are deliberate words chosen by successful people and delivered to an impressionable audience at a critical time in the lives of its members. Among the best I have ever come across was one by Apple cofounder Steve Jobs, given at Stanford University in June 2005. At the time, Jobs had overcome cancer for the time being but was reflective on life and the short amount of time we have on this earth. He shared the following words toward the end of his speech to highlight the importance of being your authentic self: "Your time is limited, so don't waste it living someone else's life. Don't be trapped by dogma—which is living with the results of other people's thinking. Don't let the noise of others' opinions drown out your own inner voice. And most important, have the courage to follow your heart and intuition. They somehow already know what you truly want to become. Everything else is secondary."

The Bottom Line: Great leaders carry themselves in an authentic way regardless of what they are doing or who they are dealing with. You can certainly adapt to any setting while remaining true to your authentic self.

Key Points:

- Understand who you are as a person and embrace it. Be transparent and be your authentic self everywhere.
- Not everyone is going to like the way you carry yourself. Don't blindly give in to them, but rather believe in who you are and be careful who you solicit advice from.
- Incorporate your passions and strengths into the leadership of yourself and others, as it will bring out the best in you, those around you, and organizations you are striving to improve.

Leading Yourself: Develop a strong understanding of who you are, fully embrace it, and be authentic 24-7. Don't try to be someone else or be who you think you need to be.

Leading Others: As a leader, create an environment in which people can be their authentic selves and share how they feel without fear of rejection or ridicule.

5. Be a Problem Solver

Leaders think and talk about the solutions.

Followers think and talk about the problems.

—Brian Tracy

The minds of great leaders work differently than those of followers. The minds of great leaders are able to identify problems and look for ways to solve them. Sometimes these are simple solutions, and other times they are radical innovations, but they always start with solving a problem. Leaders don't shy away from problems, deflect responsibility, or make up excuses. Doing those things will cause you to lose credibility with those around you. This can be applicable to a small conflict within an organization or to changing the way an entire industry functions. As a leader, constantly try to solve the problems around you and help others you lead to do the same. Leaders are consistently improving the people, organizations, and communities around them; they accomplish this by finding a problem and solving it with a better solution. Some people like to sit around complaining, blaming others, making excuses, feeling sorry for themselves, or just waiting for something to magically happen. Leaders' minds, however, are racing with ways to make things better; great leaders are problem solvers.

When I was a teenager, I solved a problem with an entrepreneurial solution that was both innovative and totally illegal. At the time, the only way to watch old television episodes was through reruns. It took a lot of hard work, but I managed to record on VHS tape (google it if you don't know what they are) every episode of *Saved by the Bell*, used a double VCR to put them all in sequential order with the commercials removed, and sold them on eBay as a boxed set of tapes. I'm not advising you to break the law, but I share this to illustrate the idea of identifying a problem and then creating a solution for it. At the time, I didn't understand a ton about business, but, looking back, I realize it was the most profitable business I'll ever run because I had zero expenses and 100 percent profitability. I was "borrowing" all of the content, the double VCR was given to me as a gift, my grandfather bought all of the VHS tapes for me, and my mom paid for all of the shipping once they were sold on eBay. Through this experience and others I pursued over the years, I learned a great deal about business, entrepreneurship, and leadership. It wasn't so much about what I was doing as about what I was learning, which was the process of running a small business and selling a product online, skills that would serve me well in future endeavors.

During my junior year of college, I was thrown into the fire of being a problem solver, and it was an invaluable experience in my development as a leader. I was heavily involved in my fraternity and was constantly finding ways to make the organization better and improve the house we lived in. Over the years, we had officials from the city inspect our house and provide a list of modifications that were needed in order to be compliant with various building codes they required. Each year that growing list would promptly be ignored, crumpled up, and thrown away. No big deal, we would think, these were probably more friendly suggestions than actual requirements, right? In the summer prior to my junior year, the local official once again inspected our home, but this time he found significant issues, provided a huge list of items, and told us they must be fixed immediately or else we'd be in trouble. The alumni of our fraternity, who I worked closely with, brushed this off, and it was business as usual that semester.

At the conclusion of the semester, we were given final notice that either these violations would be fixed or the building would be condemned. The list of one-hundred-plus violations ended up being over $200,000 worth of work that needed to be completed by the first week of January. Otherwise, the forty-five guys who lived in the house would not be allowed to move back in. At the time, I was stressed out, overwhelmed, and felt well outside of my comfort zone. After all, I wasn't a landlord or handyman, and I hadn't had any experiences even remotely close to this. I felt like I had the weight of my fraternity brothers, their parents, the university, city officials, and our national fraternity all on my shoulders, and I knew that moment was the biggest test I had ever faced as a leader. Once the initial shock wore off, I thought to myself that, regardless of the outcome, this would be a tremendous learning experience that I should embrace with a positive attitude and give my absolute best. If I did these things, I knew I would be able to hold my head high at the end because I had done everything I could.

It turned out to be an unbelievable amount of work to project manage all of these home improvements while also coordinating communication with all parties involved. To make matters worse, the improvements still weren't done by the time school started in January. So, I had to relocate forty-five guys to various places around campus and explain to many of their parents why they were paying rent for a house and yet their son was sleeping on a couch a mile away. The end result was that everything was fixed, the guys moved back into the house, and the entire experience made me a significantly better leader. The lesson here is to embrace problems head on, roll up your sleeves, and solve them. I could have avoided responsibility, but the problem wouldn't have been solved, and, just as importantly, I would have missed out on an incredible opportunity to improve as a leader. I was able to use the lessons from that experience in many ways during the following years. I also felt substantially more confidence moving forward as a leader because I had a better sense of what I was capable of in a time of crisis.

A great example of a problem solver is Blake Mycoskie, founder of TOMS Shoes. In his twenties he started and sold multiple companies, showing that he was well suited for an entrepreneurial career. While traveling through Argentina in 2006, he noticed children in the area were so poor they didn't even have shoes, and many of them had blisters, sores, and infections on their feet. After seeing this problem firsthand, he came up with a revolutionary solution: to create a for-profit, "one-for-one" business. For every pair of TOMS Shoes sold, one pair would be donated to children in need of shoes. This business turned into a global movement, and Mycoskie continued to solve additional problems. TOMS Shoes has provided over 60 million pairs of shoes to children since 2006; TOMS Eyewear has restored sight to over 400,000 people since 2011; and TOMS Roasting Company has helped provide over 335,000 weeks of safe water since launching in 2014. In 2015, TOMS Bag Collection was founded with the mission to help provide training for skilled birth attendants and distribute birth kits containing items that help a woman safely deliver her baby. So far, safe birth services have been provided for over 25,000 mothers. Mycoskie continues looking for new problems to solve. As he says, "The goal isn't how much money you make, but how much you help people."

There is a huge difference between leaders who solve problems and those who shy away from them. A great example of this is the same person acting much different in two different situations; this example will illustrate the difference between solving a problem and avoiding a problem. President George W. Bush was leading our country when 9/11 happened in 2001. One of the most iconic moments in recent history came just three days after the attacks when Bush was standing on the rubble at Ground Zero. He grabbed a bullhorn and started thanking the police, firefighters, and first responders for all of their hard work. When someone in the crowd yelled that they couldn't hear him, he declared, "I can hear you! The rest of the world hears you! And the people—and the people who knocked these buildings down will hear all of us soon." The crowd went wild and started loudly chanting, "U-S-A, U-S-A!" This moment was a great display of a leader taking ownership of a problem and attempting to solve it. His 90 percent approval rating as president was through the roof because people of all political views respected his leadership in the moment.

Fast-forward to 2005 and another pivotal moment in his presidency. On August 23, Hurricane Katrina hit the Gulf Coast. President Bush, in another iconic moment, was famously pictured flying over the hurricane damage in Air Force One. But they did not land the plane for him to visit the men and women beginning to fix the devastation the storm had caused. Bush clearly stated that the reason for not landing the plane was that it would have been a distraction from the clean-up efforts. It didn't matter, though. The perception among the people was that he was avoiding the problem and not doing his best to solve it. His popularity had certainly worn off from 9/11, but it took an even larger hit because of his handling of this situation. His approval rating reached as low as 34 percent in some polls. A major reason for the public's frustration with him in this instance is that they perceived he wasn't doing his absolute best to solve the problem at hand. People want to see their leaders do everything in their power to solve problems; you can clearly see the difference here in how you are viewed when you actively solve a problem versus how you are viewed when you either avoid the problem outright or give the appearance that you are avoiding it.

In 1994 a rising young executive in the New York City finance industry decided to quit his lucrative job, move to Seattle, and fix what he saw as a problem in the book industry. His vision was to start selling books on the Internet, something that had never really been done before. It was a difficult decision for him to make, and many in his life warned him that it would be a bad idea. He ultimately attributed his reason for doing it to, as he called it, a "regret minimization framework." He looked out to being eighty years old and wondered if he would regret not giving this radical idea a shot. He identified a problem (the increasingly antiquated book industry), had a vision for what he wanted to achieve (selling books on the Internet), was confident in the steps he needed to take to make it a reality (a detailed business plan), and had full confidence going for it because he knew he would regret it if he didn't try. Jeff Bezos has grown Amazon to a company that sells virtually everything online and is worth over $200 billion.

Once he conquered selling books online, he looked to solve an even larger problem, as successful people do, and shifted Amazon's focus "to be the earth's most customer-centric company; to build a place where people can come to find and discover anything they might want to buy online." Successful leaders are constantly looking for bigger and bigger problems to solve. As Bezos puts it, "My view is there's no bad time to innovate."

As Gianni Versace, founder of Versace, once said, "In the past, people were born royal. Nowadays, royalty comes from what you do." We are constantly surrounded by problems in this world; it is your willingness and ability to solve those problems that will dictate your success as a leader.

The Bottom Line: If you want to accomplish great things as a leader, constantly look for problems and solve them.

Key Points:

- The minds of great leaders work differently than other people's as they actively look for and solve problems.

- There is a significant difference in how you are perceived as a leader when you solve problems instead of hiding from them.
- Many great accomplishments simply start with a leader identifying a problem and then solving it with a great solution.

Leading Yourself: Look around at yourself, your organizations, and your community. What problems can you solve? Pick one and get started!

Leading Others: Encourage those around you to each focus on one problem they'd like to solve to make your organization or community better; once they have identified it, do everything in your power to help them solve it.

6. Always Persevere

Tough times never last, but tough people do.

—Robert H. Schuller

One of the things that is certain in life is that you will face adversity. It is an absolute given. You have two options when you face adversity: either you quit or you persevere. It truly is that simple. You will face adversity in your life; your friends and family will face adversity in their lives; and any organization you are involved with will face adversity as well. So, prepare to constantly be looking adversity in the eye. If you learn how to accept adversity, challenges, and setbacks in a calm and positive way, it will serve you extremely well throughout your life. Getting knocked down isn't a big deal; it is how quickly you can stand back up that matters. Look at any successful person in this world. I promise you that person faced plenty of adversity on their road to success, but they ultimately persevered through all of the challenges they faced.

If leadership was easy, then everyone would thrive at it and it wouldn't be such a sought-after characteristic. The reason leadership is difficult is because a key component of it is being able to persevere through challenges, whether they are something you personally are facing or something an entire organization is up against. It is your ability to push through the challenges that plays a large part in your ability as a leader. As a French proverb says, "One may go a long way after one is tired." We all have a ridiculous amount of potential in us, but it is our responsibility to tap into it. One of the ways we truly reach our potential is to constantly persevere through every challenge thrown at us. What happens when things don't initially go our way? We reverse course, develop a new strategy, and get back after it.

Writing my first book was not an easy process, and it did not happen quickly. For well over a year, I worked seven days a week and did nothing that resembled a break or vacation. I'd wake up most days at five o'clock and head to my local Starbucks, where I'd sit in the same corner seat working on the book. During the day, I'd go do my day job to make sure I was able to pay my bills, or at least do my best to come close. At night I'd get back to work on writing my book until I was no longer productive and needed sleep. After many edits, I had created a draft that I was proud of. The final step was a great opportunity to share the draft with a family friend who was a professional editor. She said she was happy to edit the book if I sent a printed manuscript in the mail, and I took her up on her offer.

A few weeks passed, and I received a package from her with the edited book. As you can probably imagine, I was thrilled to receive this, because it was the final step before getting my book published. I took the package into my room, ripped it open, and anxiously thumbed through the pages of red-ink edits. Quickly I realized that after the first few pages, there were no more red-ink marks. My initial thought was that maybe the rest of the book was perfect, but I quickly remembered how poor my grammar was and knew that couldn't possibly be the case. I then noticed a note on her personal stationery sitting in the box, and I grabbed the note and read it through. The note she wrote me said that I shouldn't move forward with this book and that I wasn't ready to write it. Her suggestion was to put the book in my desk drawer and attempt to write it again when I turned thirty, which was seven years down the road. The roughly ninety seconds after reading that note was probably the lowest point of my twenties. I felt this incredibly sick feeling of being an absolute failure. I'm not sure what exactly went through my mind, but after those ninety seconds I made the decision that I was going to refuse to take this advice and would make it my mission to prove her wrong. For years I used this note as motivation and would carry it around the country with me as I was traveling to speak on college campuses.

Ultimately, I chose not to take her advice because I had too strong a belief in my professional vision and I was too determined to let anyone talk me out of it. As I said earlier, sometimes you take advice and sometimes you politely ignore it. This was an instance in which I correctly chose not to take it. The lesson here is to always persevere, because life is filled with negativity, setbacks, and people telling you what you can't do. If you believe in something, then put your head down, give it 100 percent, and never look back; the worst case is failure, something we will all experience in our lives. I'd much rather look my friends and family in the eye and say "I failed" than say "I didn't even try."

Less than six months after I had finished my book and launched a professional speaking career, it was the holiday season, and I was back home in Pittsburgh. At a local charity event in our community, I began talking to a family friend who had entrepreneurial experience. I shared with him what I was working on and my vision for what I wanted to do in my new career. After I shared this with him I anxiously waited for his words of encouragement and his offer to help in any way he could. Instead, and I'll never forget this, he looked at me and said, "You are way too young to do something like that. Nobody will find you credible, and I don't know who would listen to you." Things like this were not easy to hear, and as I look back I can only wonder: if this is what people were saying to my face as I got started, what in the heck were they saying behind my back?

There is a quote from Mark Twain I wish I had read during the challenges I had while establishing myself professionally: "Keep away from people who belittle your ambitions. Small people always do that, but the really great make you feel that you, too, can become great." Whether it was the family friend, the editor who told me to not write my book, or one of the countless others who told me all the reasons why I couldn't succeed, it took a great deal of perseverance to fight through all of the negativity. How was I able to do it? My family gave me the strength and encouragement to believe I could do anything. Along with that they gave me lessons on the hard work and perseverance it takes to actually succeed in this world. If you don't have the attitude of perseverance, it can be challenging to fight through the garbage negative people throw at you.

Great leaders also have the unique ability to help others believe in themselves far more than they could on their own. Have the attitude of perseverance, and instill that in everyone around you, because it is challenging for people or organizations to experience sustainable success without a constant willingness to persevere through adversity. You have the opportunity as a leader to change the perspectives of other people, to help them become more positive and ultimately have an attitude of perseverance. Will you always be successful? Of course not, but you can certainly do your best to try.

It is important to remember that it isn't where you start that matters; it is where you end up. Take, for example, Sonia Sotomayor, who was raised by Puerto Rican–born parents in the Bronx, certainly not the most upscale area of New York City. At the age of nine, she lost her father and was raised by her mother. Despite not having a head start or any "luck," she managed to work her way up to being on the US Supreme Court, a designation only nine people in our country can hold at once. Do you think it might have been difficult for a female of Hispanic heritage to persevere all the way to the US Supreme Court? Of course it was, but she had the attitude it takes to overcome anything. As she said, "I have never had to face anything that could overwhelm the native optimism and stubborn perseverance I was blessed with." Regardless of the criticism and obstacles she faced, and there were plenty, she continually persevered through all of it. She never felt sorry for herself or made excuses for why she couldn't accomplish everything she wanted to in this world. So much of life is how you look at it. She constantly took the "glass half-full" approach and remained optimistic every step of the way. Do some people start off in more challenging situations than others in life? Absolutely. Life isn't always fair.

A young girl growing up in poverty-stricken rural Mississippi was so poor that she had to wear dresses made of potato sacks, which led to ridicule from her classmates. She was initially raised by her mother, a teenager herself, before bouncing around to various homes. As a child, she was sexually abused by multiple family members. After years of abuse she decided to run away from home. At fourteen years old, she became pregnant and subsequently lost the child in infancy. It was a challenging beginning to her life, without a doubt.

This young lady would eventually begin to turn her life around by earning an opportunity to work on the radio while in high school and to anchor the local evening news at the age of just nineteen. Her hard work led to a syndicated television show, *The Oprah Winfrey Show*, that became the highest-rated program of its kind in history. Oprah's success did not come as a shock to her; as she said, "I always knew I was destined for greatness." She would go on to entertain, educate, and empower millions of people through her television show and to become one of the world's greatest philanthropists. In her words, "I don't think of myself as a poor, deprived ghetto girl who made good. I think of myself as somebody who from an early age knew I was responsible for myself, and I had to make good." The lesson from Oprah's remarkable life is to accept responsibility for yourself, regardless of what situation you find yourself in, and then persevere until you achieve the greatness you desire. Along the way, she also learned the power of authenticity, saying "I had no idea that being your authentic self could make me as rich as I've become. If I had, I'd have done it a lot earlier."

Everyone knows who Walt Disney is and the empire that he created, but few know the ridiculous amount of perseverance it took for him to thrive as a leader. When he was starting out his career, he was fired from the *Kansas City Star* newspaper because his boss believed he "lacked creativity." He persevered through that by starting his own animation company in 1921 by raising money from investors. Unfortunately, he made a deal with a distributor who went out of business, and he was forced to close down his company. As a result, he was barely able to pay his rent and was eating dog food for meals.

Disney once again persevered, this time pulling together his last few dollars and purchasing a train ticket to Hollywood. He was about to face more adversity, however. He had created a cartoon character named Oswald the Rabbit that Universal Studios (its distributor) had secretly patented. This led to Universal using the character without Disney involved with it or compensated for any of it. Do you think most people might have just given up by this point?

Disney continued to face adversity. Another recently created character called Mickey Mouse was rejected because it would "terrify women." He was also in the middle of producing *Pinocchio* when they made him shut the operation down and rewrite the entire storyline. As if all of this wasn't enough, Disney faced possibly his greatest uphill battle in trying to turn the book *Mary Poppins* into a film. *Mary Poppins* was written by an author named Pamela Travers, who had zero interest in selling her book to Hollywood to make a movie. Disney proceeded to visit her in England repeatedly over a sixteen-year period before she finally agreed to let him make a movie out of her book. The result of Disney's perseverance is greatness that has entertained millions of people around the world and created an empire worth over $180 billion that employs almost two hundred thousand people. None of that would have been possible had a young man not been willing to persevere through an unbelievable amount of adversity. Disney embraced his challenges, saying,

"All the adversity I've had in my life, all my troubles and obstacles, have strengthened me. You may not realize it when it happens, but a kick in the teeth may be the best thing in the world for you." Disney passed away in 1966, but thirty years later the company he built bought ABC, which owned the *Kansas City Star*, meaning that the newspaper that fired him ended up being bought by the empire he created.

As a child, Fred Smith was born with a hip disorder called Calve-Perthes disease, which caused him to wear braces and walk with crutches throughout his youth. He was eventually able to overcome this and work his way into Yale University, a prestigious Ivy League school. While taking an economics class, he wrote a paper on an idea he had had for a new business in which packages would be able to be delivered overnight utilizing computer technology. His professor looked at the paper and told him he could get a C if the "idea was actually feasible."

Many people would have received that feedback and never pursued the idea. After all, an Ivy League professor told him the idea was not feasible. Fortunately, Fred Smith didn't give up, saying, "I'm not afraid to take a swing and miss." His perseverance would lead to what became known as FedEx, which forever changed the way business was done on a variety of levels. As with most other successful businesses, FedEx took years of hard work and perseverance, including one time when the company almost went bankrupt. Smith took the final $5,000 the company had to Las Vegas, turned it into $27,000 playing blackjack, and was able to pay the company's $24,000 fuel bill. The result of Smith's perseverance is recognition among the world's greatest leaders, a personal net worth of over $700 million, and a company worth over $40 billion, one that was deemed "not feasible" by a professor.

There is a Japanese proverb that says, "Fall seven times, stand up eight." A great example of this proverb in action involves a woman with a book manuscript that she thought was excellent but that twelve different publishers did not. While she was in the process of writing this book, she described her life as a mess, was going through a divorce, and lived in a tiny flat with her daughter. As she put it, "There was a point where I really felt I had 'penniless divorcee lone parent' tattooed on my head." She was surviving on government subsidies, and her mother had also just recently passed away. Despite all of this, she continued to spend the majority of her free time working on her book series and drew on many of her bad experiences in her writing. After twelve different publishers rejected her, she finally found a small one that was willing to publish her work despite telling her to get a day job, which was a real show of faith in her book! With all of the adversity she was facing, you could certainly understand why she would want to give up. But successful people refuse to give up. What was the result of J. K. Rowling's perseverance? A book series starring Harry Potter that is currently worth nearly $15 billion, with more than 450 million books sold. It isn't about how many times you fall down; it is about how many times you stand back up.

The Bottom Line: Successful leaders should strive to constantly persevere, as it pays off to fight through the inevitable adversity you will face to accomplish whatever you want to in this world.

Key Points:

- Successful leaders handle adversity with a positive attitude and a desire to fight through things without making excuses, feeling sorry for themselves, or giving up.
- As a leader, you will encounter people who give up easily, have a "glass half-empty" attitude about things, and can't handle adversity. Your challenge is to pick them up, brush them off, and help them persevere moving forward.
- Everyone faces setbacks, challenges, and moments of adversity. It isn't about how many times you fall down but about how many times you get back up.

Leading Yourself: Think about the last setback you had, how you could have handled it differently, and what you will do in the future to combat adversity with perseverance.

Leading Others: Determine what you will do when you see someone dealing with a challenge. How will you help that person overcome adversity with a persevering attitude?

Taking Action

As I said at the beginning, the point of this book isn't just for you to understand leadership; it is also for you to actually lead. For this information to positively impact you, you must take action. Here is how you can take action on the key points we covered.

Be the hardest worker in the room. Outwork everyone around you, and help others understand the value of hard work.

Have a laser-focused vision. Know what you want for your future. Work with others to develop strong visions for organizations you are involved with.

Surround yourself with good people. Build an army of good people to make you a better leader, and constantly work to connect good people and organizations with each other.

Be authentic 24-7. Be your authentic self, and encourage others to be comfortable doing the same.

Be a problem solver. Create solutions for the problems around you, and make sure organizations you are involved with have the same attitude.

Always persevere. Fight through whatever life throws your way, and help those around you fight through adversity as well.

Years ago, my favorite teacher, Mrs. Natali, gave me a copy of Dr. Seuss's *Oh, the Places You'll Go*, which is a great book that allows us to reflect on our lives and where we are headed. One passage in particular always stands out to me because it articulates how we control our own destiny and can lead ourselves wherever we want:

> *You have brains in your head.*
> *You have feet in your shoes.*
> *You can steer yourself*
> *any direction you choose.*

It is easy in life to lose sight of the simple fact that we can lead ourselves in whatever direction we choose, so choose wisely! Too many people go through life wishing and hoping instead of doing. Embrace every opportunity you have to lead yourself, lead others, make the community around you better, continue learning, spend time with loved ones, meet amazing people, have an incredible social life, take care of yourself both physically and mentally, experience new things, and do anything else that will make your life more enjoyable and meaningful.

Beginning now, commit to thriving in everything you do. Leadership is truly limitless once you tap into your extraordinary potential!

To contact or learn more about Tom Healy:

www.tom-healy.com

tom@tom-healy.com

Facebook, Twitter, Instagram & LinkedIn:

TomHealySays

Made in the USA
Lexington, KY
09 September 2016

55099425R00060